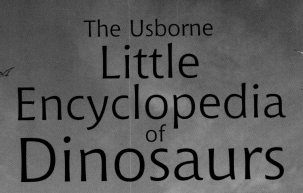

The Usborne
Little
Encyclopedia
of
Dinosaurs

Sam Taplin

Designed by Keith Newell
and Mark Franklin

Illustrated by David Hancock

Consultant: Professor Michael Benton

Using Internet links

Throughout this book we have suggested interesting websites where you can find out more about dinosaurs. To visit the sites, go to the Usborne Quicklinks Website at **www.usborne-quicklinks.com** and type the keywords "little dinosaurs". Here are some of the things you can do on the websites:

• Watch amazing video clips of dinosaurs

• Print out pictures of prehistoric animals

• Listen to how dinosaurs may have sounded

• Go on adventures in the prehistoric world

Internet safety

When using the Internet, please make sure you follow these guidelines:

• Ask your parent's or guardian's permission before you connect to the Internet.

• If you write a message in a website guest book or on a website message board, do not include any personal information such as your full name, address or telephone number, and ask an adult before you give your email address.

• Never arrange to meet anyone you have talked to on the Internet.

• If a website asks you to log in or register by typing your name or email address, ask permission from an adult first.

• If you do receive an email from someone you don't know, tell an adult and do not reply to the email.

Computer not essential

If you don't have access to the Internet, don't worry. This book is a complete, self-contained reference book on its own.

Site availability

The links in Usborne Quicklinks are regularly reviewed and updated, but occasionally, you may get a message that a site is unavailable. This might be temporary, so try again later, or even the next day. Websites do occasionally close down and when this happens, we will replace them with new links in Usborne Quicklinks. Sometimes we add extra links too, if we think they are useful. So when you visit Usborne Quicklinks, the links may be slightly different from those described in your book.

Downloadable pictures

Pictures in this book marked with a ★ symbol can be downloaded from Usborne Quicklinks for your own personal use, for example, to illustrate a homework report or project. The pictures are the copyright of Usborne Publishing and may not be used for any commercial or profit-related purpose. To download a picture, go to Usborne Quicklinks and follow the instructions there.

Notes for parents and guardians

The websites described in this book are regularly reviewed and the links in Usborne Quicklinks are updated. However, the content of a website may change at any time and Usborne Publishing is not responsible for the content on any website other than its own. We recommend that children are supervised while on the Internet, that they do not use Internet chat rooms, and that you use Internet filtering software to block unsuitable material. Please ensure that your children read and follow the safety guidelines printed on the left. For more information, see the "Net Help" area on the Usborne Quicklinks Website.

To go to all the websites described in this book, go to **www.usborne-quicklinks.com** and enter the keywords "little dinosaurs".

Contents

This picture shows a pair of meat-eating raptors creeping up on a group of hadrosaurs.

To hear how to say the names of the creatures in this book, go to **www.usborne-quicklinks.com**

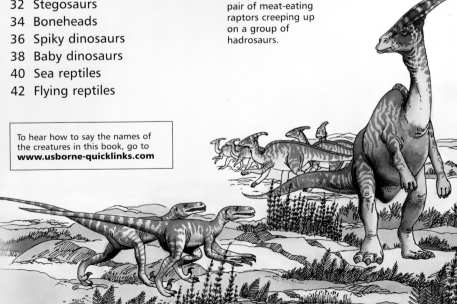

The prehistoric world

There were animals on Earth long before there were any people. These animals are called prehistoric animals. The most famous ones are the dinosaurs.

This picture shows when different prehistoric animals lived. You can also see which pages to turn to for more information.

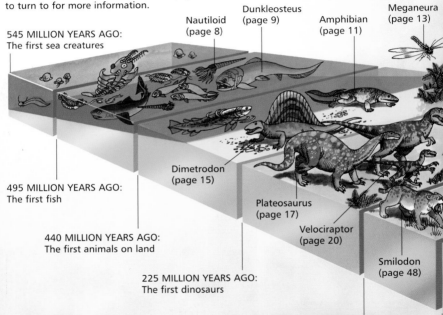

Nautiloid (page 8)

Dunkleosteus (page 9)

Amphibian (page 11)

Meganeura (page 13)

545 MILLION YEARS AGO:
The first sea creatures

495 MILLION YEARS AGO:
The first fish

Dimetrodon (page 15)

440 MILLION YEARS AGO:
The first animals on land

Plateosaurus (page 17)

Velociraptor (page 20)

225 MILLION YEARS AGO:
The first dinosaurs

Smilodon (page 48)

50 MILLION YEARS AGO:
The first horses, elephants, cats and dogs

Different dinosaurs

There were many different shapes and sizes of dinosaurs. Some were the biggest creatures ever to walk on the Earth, but others were as small as hens. There were peaceful plant-eaters, and fierce meat-eaters that hunted other dinosaurs.

2 MILLION YEARS AGO:
The first people

Other animals

Lots of other animals lived at the same time as the dinosaurs. Some had leathery wings and went flapping through the sky. Others lived deep in the sea. There were also crocodiles, turtles, insects and small, furry animals.

Today's crocodiles look very like the crocodiles of prehistoric times.

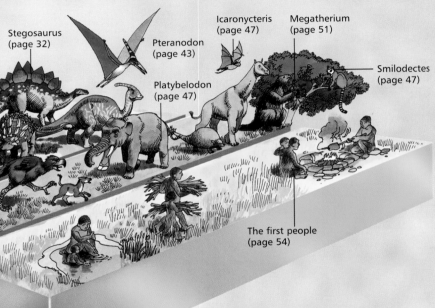

Stegosaurus (page 32)

Pteranodon (page 43)

Icaronycteris (page 47)

Megatherium (page 51)

Platybelodon (page 47)

Smilodectes (page 47)

The first people (page 54)

Different times

Different prehistoric animals lived at different times. As time passed, some types of animals died out and new ones appeared. Most kinds of prehistoric animals died out millions of years ago. But some present-day animals, such as turtles, have hardly changed since prehistoric times.

Internet link

For a link to a website where you can find out about different periods of prehistoric time, go to **www.usborne-quicklinks.com**

How the Earth began

Scientists think the Earth was formed 4,600 million years ago. For millions of years, there was no life on Earth. The whole planet was dry and rocky.

1. The Earth was formed from dust and gases whirling around the Sun.

2. The gas cloud became incredibly hot and changed into a ball of liquid rock.

3. Slowly, the rock cooled down. A layer of solid rock formed around the outside.

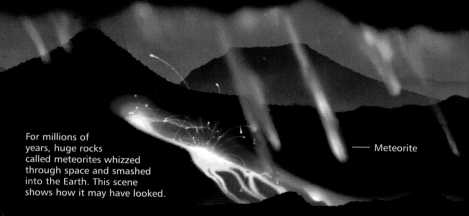

For millions of years, huge rocks called meteorites whizzed through space and smashed into the Earth. This scene shows how it may have looked.

—— Meteorite

Volcanoes poured out red-hot liquid rock (lava) onto the surface of the Earth.

The first oceans

Thick clouds surrounded the Earth. About 3,500 million years ago, rain began to fall. It poured with rain for thousands of years and this rainwater formed the Earth's oceans and rivers.

Internet link

For a link to a website where you can see video clips of volcanoes pouring out liquid rock, go to **www.usborne-quicklinks.com**

The first living things

Life began in the oceans. The first living things were incredibly tiny and simple. They were a little like germs. Very slowly, these tiny living things changed and became bigger and more complicated.

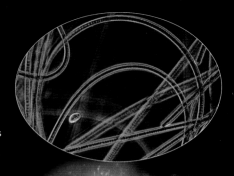

By 545 million years ago, plants and animals were living in the sea. Blue-green algae like these were some of the first plants.

Volcano

Lava flowing across the ground

A changing world

The Earth looked very different in prehistoric times. Since the world began, the land has been moving around on the Earth's surface. 250 million years ago, all the land came together to make one big continent.

Pangaea

250 million years ago, the land formed a huge continent called Pangaea.

Then, Pangaea split apart. This is how the Earth looked 60 million years ago.

Under the sea

By 545 million years ago, the oceans were swarming with hundreds of amazing creatures. Some of these creatures looked nothing like any animal alive today.

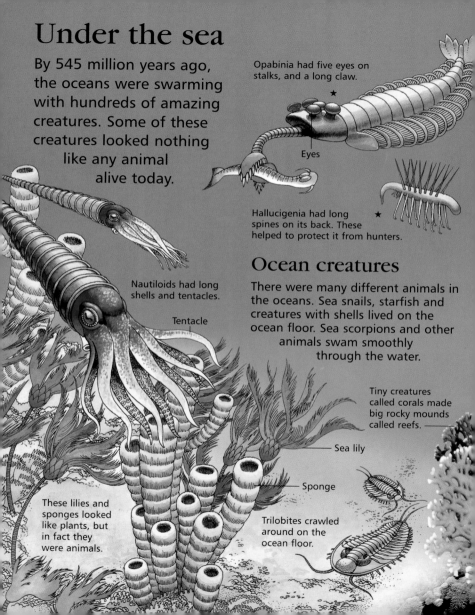

Opabinia had five eyes on stalks, and a long claw.

Eyes

Hallucigenia had long spines on its back. These helped to protect it from hunters.

Nautiloids had long shells and tentacles.

Tentacle

Ocean creatures

There were many different animals in the oceans. Sea snails, starfish and creatures with shells lived on the ocean floor. Sea scorpions and other animals swam smoothly through the water.

Tiny creatures called corals made big rocky mounds called reefs.

Sea lily

Sponge

These lilies and sponges looked like plants, but in fact they were animals.

Trilobites crawled around on the ocean floor.

The first fish

The first fish had no jaws or teeth. They had to suck up their food from the seabed. Later fish had powerful jaws and sharp teeth. This meant they could eat lots of other foods.

Deadly hunters

Some sea creatures were expert hunters who chased and ate other animals. The animals they ate had hard shells, scales and spikes to protect themselves from the hunters.

Internet link

For a link to a website where you can watch video clips of prehistoric sharks, go to **www.usborne-quicklinks.com**

Some fish were enormous.
★ Dunkleosteus was as long as a bus.

These fish had spines on their fins. This made them difficult to eat.

Sea scorpions were some of the deadliest hunters. They had sharp pincers for catching animals.

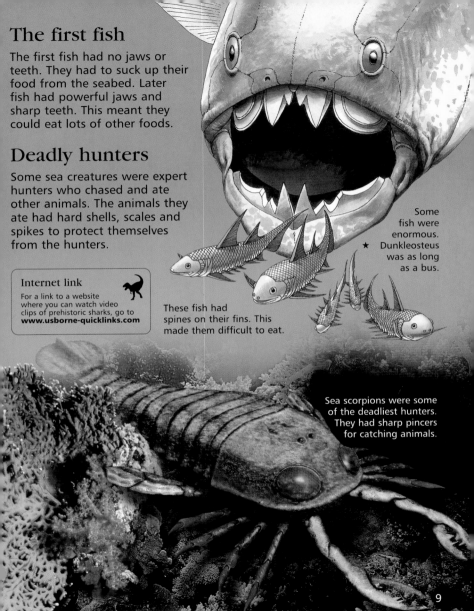

Life on the land

For millions of years, nothing lived on the land. The first plants and animals appeared there around 440 million years ago.

The scene on these two pages shows some of the first land plants and animals.

The first land plants

The first plants on the land needed lots of water to survive. They grew in wet, marshy places near the sea. Later plants grew in drier places, and they spread out over the rest of the land.

Internet link
For a link to a website with a clickable timeline of life on Earth, go to
www.usborne-quicklinks.com

Like many of the first plants, Rhynia had no leaves.

Land and water

Some fish lived in shallow water and had two big fins at the front of their body and two at the back. Very slowly, these four fins turned into legs. These new four-legged animals were called amphibians.

These pictures show how some fish's fins turned into legs. This took millions of years.

This is a prehistoric fish with four strong fins. It used its front fins to push its head out of the water.

Back fin

Front fin

Land animals

Once there were plants on land, there was food for animals to eat. Some of the first creatures that lived on land were snails, centipedes, spiders and insects.

Insects sucked food from inside plants.

Spider-like creatures ate insects.

Gigantoscorpio was a scorpion as big as a dog. It had a large, stinging tail.

Millipedes ate rotting plants.

This fish-like creature had four legs. It could push itself around in shallow water.

This is one of the first amphibians. Amphibians live partly on the land and partly in the water.

Fishy tail for swimming

11

Swampy forests

About 350 million years ago, large parts of the world were covered in swamps. Plants grew very well in these wet places. Huge forests of giant trees sprang up there.

Swamp creatures

The forests were full of huge bugs and spiders. Giant dragonflies flew between the trees. These were the first creatures with wings. Lots of animals called amphibians lived there too.

This scene shows plants and creatures in a swampy forest.

Enormous spiders spun webs to catch insects.

Giant millipedes crawled through the leaves on the forest floor.

Ophiderpeton was a snake-like amphibian.

Big, fierce amphibians lived in the swamps and hunted fish. This is Pholidogaster.

Diplocaulus was an amphibian with strange fins on its head.

Trees were much taller than most trees today. Some were as high as a building with 12 floors.

Internet link

For a link to a website where you can learn about the animals that live in swamps today, go to **www.usborne-quicklinks.com**

This is Meganeura, a dragonfly as big as a seagull.

Ferns

Making coal

Dead plants and fallen trees covered the forest floor. Very slowly, they were buried under layers of heavy mud. The mud squeezed down hard on the plants and squashed them. Over millions of years, the squashed plants became coal.

This picture shows how coal is formed.

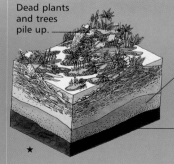

Dead plants and trees pile up.

Plants and trees are squeezed by mud. They turn into squashy brown peat.

Peat is squeezed and turned into hard black coal.

★

The first reptiles

About 300 million years ago, creatures called reptiles were living on the land. Earlier animals had to spend part of their time in the water, but reptiles could stay on land all the time.

Hylonomus was one of the first reptiles. It looked like a lizard.

Internet link

For a link to a website where you can paint and print out a picture of Dimetrodon, go to **www.usborne-quicklinks.com**

What is a reptile?

Reptiles are still around today. All reptiles have hard, scaly skin and are cold-blooded. This means their bodies don't make heat. They need heat from the Sun to keep them warm and give them energy. Tortoises and lizards are reptiles.

On the left is a modern-day lizard from South America, called an iguana.

— Scaly skin

All reptiles lay eggs. Here you can see a baby tortoise hatching from its egg.

All kinds of reptiles

Some prehistoric reptiles looked like today's reptiles, but others were very different. Some were big and strong, while others were small and thin. Some ate plants and some hunted other animals.

Moschops was a plant-eating reptile the size of a hippopotamus.

★

Lycaenops was a small, fast-moving reptile that hunted in a pack.

Dimetrodon had a big sail of bone and skin on its back. It may have used its sail to soak up heat from the Sun.

★

Big, sharp teeth for tearing up meat

The first dinosaurs

The first dinosaurs appeared on the Earth about 225 million years ago. Dinosaurs were a new kind of reptile.

Long legs

Dinosaurs had much longer and stronger legs than other prehistoric reptiles. This made some dinosaurs extremely fast runners.

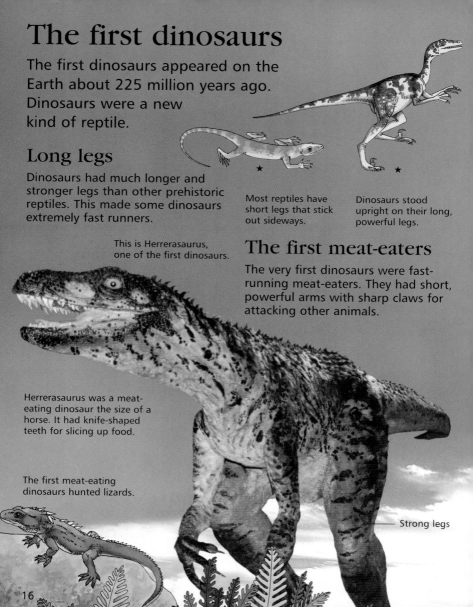

Most reptiles have short legs that stick out sideways.

Dinosaurs stood upright on their long, powerful legs.

This is Herrerasaurus, one of the first dinosaurs.

The first meat-eaters

The very first dinosaurs were fast-running meat-eaters. They had short, powerful arms with sharp claws for attacking other animals.

Herrerasaurus was a meat-eating dinosaur the size of a horse. It had knife-shaped teeth for slicing up food.

The first meat-eating dinosaurs hunted lizards.

Strong legs

Internet link

For a link to a website where you can find out more about early dinosaurs and their world, go to **www.usborne-quicklinks.com**

The first plant-eaters

Other dinosaurs ate plants instead of meat. They were bigger than the meat-eaters and they lived in groups, or herds. The plant-eaters walked on four legs, but they could also stand up on their back legs to eat leaves high up in the trees.

This is Plateosaurus, one of the first plant-eating dinosaurs. From nose to tail, it was as long as four people lying end to end.

Beak-like mouth for munching leaves

Claws for holding onto trees

Mighty reptiles

Soon there were lots of different kinds of dinosaurs. The biggest ones were huge and powerful. For 160 million years, dinosaurs were the strongest and fastest animals on the Earth.

17

Hunter dinosaurs

There were many kinds of meat-eating dinosaurs. Some were huge, but others were as small as cats. They all walked on their back legs and were expert hunters.

Compsognathus was one of the smallest meat-eaters. It hunted insects and other tiny creatures.

Spinosaurus had long jaws, like a crocodile. It may have hunted fish from rivers.

Fast and deadly

One of the fiercest hunters was a fast-moving dinosaur called Coelophysis. It had a thin body with very light bones. This meant it didn't have much weight to carry around, so it could run very fast.

Coelophysis attacked by charging quickly at its enemies. It slashed them with its deadly claws and teeth.

— Long claws

Warming eggs

A meat-eater called Oviraptor looked after its eggs, like a bird. It sat on the eggs to keep them warm until its babies hatched out. (For more about dinosaur eggs, see page 38.)

Here you can see an Oviraptor sitting on its nest to keep its eggs warm.

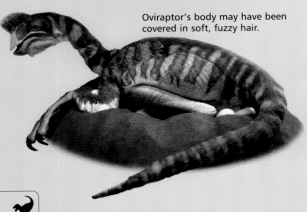

Oviraptor's body may have been covered in soft, fuzzy hair.

Internet link

For a link to a website where you can go hunting with the meat-eating dinosaur Coelophysis, go to **www.usborne-quicklinks.com**

Ostrich dinosaurs

One group of hunters had long necks and beaks. They looked a little like large birds such as ostriches, and they are known as ostrich dinosaurs. They were fast runners and they chased lizards and insects.

Ostrich dinosaurs could run much faster than the quickest athletes in the world today.

Ostrich dinosaurs weren't as fierce as other meat-eaters. But they could easily run away from bigger dinosaurs.

Powerful back legs for running fast

The dinosaurs' long tails helped them to balance while running.

Raptors

Some of the fiercest meat-eating dinosaurs were the dromaeosaurs, or raptors. They weren't as big as some other meat-eaters, but they were deadly killers.

This is a huge raptor called Utahraptor. It was bigger than a rhino.

Killing machines

Raptors had huge, razor-sharp claws and big, jagged teeth. They were intelligent, had good eyesight and were fast runners. This made them really dangerous.

Raptors hunted in packs. These Velociraptors are attacking a big plant-eating dinosaur called Tenontosaurus.

The raptors cling onto the dinosaur with their claws.

Velociraptors had an enormous claw on each foot.

Deadly jumps

Experts think that raptors attacked by running and jumping onto other animals. As they jumped, they stuck their legs out and smashed into the animal with their claws.

Before the birds?

Most dinosaurs had scaly skin, but some raptors may have been covered in short, fluffy hair. Others may even have had feathers. Experts think that these feathered raptors eventually turned into the first birds.

This is a feathered raptor called Sinornithosaurus. It's leaping through the air to attack another animal.

Feathered dinosaurs like this one wouldn't have been able to fly.

Internet link

For a link to a website where you can find out more about Utahraptor, go to **www.usborne-quicklinks.com**

The first birds

Some kinds of dinosaurs grew feathers and began to fly. These were the first birds in the world. Very slowly, these birds changed and turned into the birds we know today.

Feathery dinosaurs

Some small dinosaurs looked very like birds. They had feathers on their bodies, arms and tails. But they couldn't fly.

This is a feathered dinosaur called Caudipteryx.

Learning to fly

It took millions of years for dinosaurs to turn into birds. No one is sure how dinosaurs began to fly. It may have happened like this.

The first feathered dinosaurs climbed trees and jumped between branches.

When dinosaurs grew more feathers, they used their wings to glide between trees.

The first birds could fly through the air by flapping their feathery wings.

Here you can see Archaeopteryx, the first bird.

Early bird

The first bird we know about is called Archaeopteryx. It had long feathers and wings, like a bird. But it also had teeth and big claws, like a dinosaur. It flew through the air chasing insects.

Pointy teeth for trapping insects

This is a piece of rock with the remains of an Archaeopteryx preserved in it. Can you see the feathers on its wings?

Archaeopteryx had a long tail. This kept it steady when it was flying through the air.

Archaeopteryx used the long claws on its wings to climb trees. Then it launched itself into the air from there.

Wings

Internet link

For a link to a website where you can find out lots more about Archaeopteryx, go to **www.usborne-quicklinks.com**

Tyrannosaurus rex

Tyrannosaurs were massive meat-eating dinosaurs that walked around on two legs.

The biggest of all was Tyrannosaurus rex, which was taller than an elephant.

Giant jaws

Tyrannosaurus rex had a more powerful bite than any animal that lives on land today. Its huge jaws were full of deadly dagger-like teeth.

Tyrannosaurs sometimes fought each other. These two are about to fight.

Long, powerful legs for charging at enemies

Internet link

For a link to a website where you can print out a flip book and watch Tyrannosaurus rex run, go to **www.usborne-quicklinks.com**

Hiding and hunting

Tyrannosaurus rex was too heavy to
run very fast when it was hunting.
Instead of chasing other dinosaurs,
it took them by surprise. First, it hid
quietly somewhere. Then it charged
out with its jaws wide open.

★

As well as hunting, Tyrannosaurus rex often
ate the remains of dead animals that it found.

Tiny arms
with sharp
claws

Tiny arms

Tyrannosaurus rex had very short
arms, and this has always puzzled
experts. Its arms weren't even long
enough to reach its mouth, so it
can't have used them for eating.
Nobody is sure what they were for

When one
tyrannosaur
killed another,
the winner
sometimes ate
part of its
enemy.

Giant dinosaurs

The biggest animals that ever lived on land were a group of dinosaurs called sauropods. These giant plant-eaters walked on four legs.

Huge!

The smallest sauropods were only the size of a car, but the biggest ones were enormous. The largest sauropod we know about is Argentinosaurus. It was as long as two tennis courts laid end to end.

Sauropods had small heads and very long necks. Their necks were useful for reaching leaves on tall trees.

Sauropods needed strong legs to carry the weight of their huge bodies.

The animals trampled plants and trees into the ground.

Staying together

Sauropods lived in big groups, or herds. When the herd moved around, the younger dinosaurs stayed in the middle of the group. The grown-ups walked on the outside to protect their babies from meat-eating dinosaurs.

Internet link

For a link to a website where you can see pictures of different sauropods, go to **www.usborne-quicklinks.com**

Herds of sauropods moved around, looking for food and water.

Long tail

Peg-like teeth for pulling leaves off trees

Baby sauropod

The largest sauropods were taller than two giraffes standing on top of each other.

Stomach stones

Sauropods had blunt teeth, so they couldn't chew their food properly. Instead, they swallowed small stones. These rattled around inside their stomachs and helped them to grind up their food.

Duck-billed dinosaurs

Some dinosaurs, called hadrosaurs, are known as duck-billed dinosaurs. This is because they had flat beaks, like a duck's bill.

Hadrosaurs could grind their jaws from side to side and from front to back. This made them very good at chewing.

Beaks and chewing

All hadrosaurs ate plants. They could chop pieces off even the toughest plants with their hard, sharp beaks. They had powerful jaws for chewing and had as many as 2,000 tiny teeth.

Crest

Incredible crests

Lots of hadrosaurs had spikes, or crests, on their heads. Some of these crests were hollow inside. Hadrosaurs may have been able to blow air through their crests to make a loud booming noise.

This hadrosaur has spotted the hunters. It makes a booming noise to warn the rest of the group.

Here you can see some hunter dinosaurs creeping up on a group of hadrosaurs.

★

Looking after babies

Herds of hadrosaurs always went back to exactly the same place each year to lay their eggs. When the babies were born, the mother looked after them carefully and brought them food.

Here you can see a hadrosaur called Maiasaura looking after her babies in their nest.

Internet link

For a link to a website where you can hear how hadrosaurs and other dinosaurs may have sounded, go to **www.usborne-quicklinks.com**

Each hadrosaur nest had up to 20 eggs inside it.

The nest is made of soil.

Baby hadrosaurs were about the size of fully-grown hens.

Horned dinosaurs

Ceratopians were enormous, plant-eating dinosaurs with horns on their heads. They also had a curved frill of bone around their necks and shoulders.

Spikes and frills

Ceratopians used their sharp horns and bony frills to defend themselves against meat-eating dinosaurs. Male ceratopians probably fought each other too.

Two ceratopians fighting each other ★

This is Triceratops, the biggest ceratopian.

Sharp, parrot-like beak for slicing through plants

Scaring away enemies

Grown-up ceratopians may have protected their babies by standing in a circle around them. They probably shook their horned heads to scare away meat-eating dinosaurs.

Here you can see a group of Triceratops. The grown-up dinosaurs are standing around their babies to keep them safe.

Baby Triceratops

This big bony frill helped to protect the dinosaur's head and neck.

Triceratops had two massive horns and one smaller one.

If you stood this horn on the ground, it would be almost as tall as a grown-up person.

Different sizes

There were lots of different ceratopians. Triceratops was as big as an elephant, but some ceratopians were only the size of horses.

Internet link

For a link to a website where you can do a quiz about Triceratops, go to **www.usborne-quicklinks.com**

Stegosaurs

Stegosaurs were large, plant-eating dinosaurs with lots of big, bony plates sticking up from their backs.

Plates and spikes

A stegosaur's pointy plates helped to protect it from meat-eating dinosaurs. Stegosaurs also had long, sharp spikes on their tails. They could swing their tails sideways to scare off attackers.

This is Stegosaurus, the biggest stegosaur.

Sharp tail spike

Internet link

For a link to a website where you can print out a picture of Stegosaurus, go to **www.usborne-quicklinks.com**

A stegosaur's back legs were longer than its front legs.

Slow and stupid

Each plate was a slightly different shape.

Stegosaurs were big and heavy, and could only move slowly. They also had very small brains. Their bodies were almost as big as a bus, but their brains were the size of a table-tennis ball.

Here you can see the size of a stegosaur's brain compared with its body.

Brain

Keeping warm

Stegosaurs may have used their plates to keep warm. When a stegosaur was feeling cold, it stood with its plates facing the Sun. The plates soaked up heat and warmed its body.

These stegosaurs are warming themselves in the sunshine.

Boneheads

Pachycephalosaurs were plant-eaters with bony domes on top of their heads. These dinosaurs are known as boneheads. Male boneheads sometimes fought each other.

Pachycephalosaurus was the biggest bonehead. Below you can see two of them fighting each other.

Boneheads had strong backs, so their bones didn't break when they smashed into other dinosaurs.

A straight, stiff tail helped boneheads to keep their balance when they were running.

Strong legs with big muscles

Head-butting

Boneheads lived in groups, or herds. Male boneheads fought each other to decide who was going to be leader of the herd. Some scientists think they did this by bashing their skulls together until the weakest dinosaur gave up.

Dangerous domes

Boneheads could use their bony domes as weapons against meat-eating dinosaurs. They charged with their heads down and smashed into their enemies with their skulls.

A bonehead charging at a meat-eating Carnotaurus

Dome of bone

The dome on Pachycephalosaurus's head was 40 times thicker than a human skull.

Stygimoloch's whole head was covered in small horns and bumps.

Stygimoloch was a bonehead with long horns on the back of its head.

Internet link

For a link to a website where you can paint a bonehead and print it out, go to **www.usborne-quicklinks.com**

Spiky dinosaurs

Ankylosaurs had lots of hard, bony spikes and plates on their bodies. This helped to protect them from meat-eating dinosaurs.

An ankylosaur's back was completely covered in plates of solid bone.

Well protected

Ankylosaurs were heavy and slow, but they were so well protected that they didn't need to run away from meat-eaters. The only way a hunter could hurt an ankylosaur was by attacking its soft stomach.

This scene shows Ankylosaurus, the biggest ankylosaur, surrounded by a group of meat-eating raptors.

Internet link

For a link to a website where you can see a different type of well-protected dinosaur, go to **www.usborne-quicklinks.com**

Terrible tails

Some ankylosaurs had massive lumps of bone on the ends of their tails. They used their tails as clubs to hit meat-eating dinosaurs.

A Tyrannosaurus rex fighting an ankylosaur called Euoplocephalus

★

Bony club

Euoplocephalus's tail club could break a dinosaur's bones.

Bony spike

Ankylosaurus crouches down on the ground to keep its soft stomach protected.

Baby dinosaurs

Baby dinosaurs grew inside eggs laid by their mothers. When they were big enough to survive outside the egg, they broke the shell and crawled out. This is called hatching.

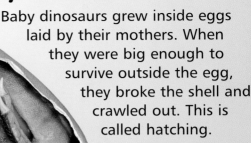

The shell is cut away so you can see inside.

Here you can see a baby dinosaur inside its egg. It isn't big enough to break out yet.

Making nests

Dinosaurs built nests to keep their eggs safe and warm. They made a mound of soil, then laid their eggs in a hole on top. They covered the eggs in leaves to keep them warm until they were ready to hatch.

Out of the egg

Some dinosaur eggshells were ten times thicker than a hen's eggshell. Baby dinosaurs had a special sharp tooth which they used to chip their way out of their eggs.

These baby Orodromeus dinosaurs have just hatched out of their eggs. You can see their leafy nest.

Growing up

Even the most enormous dinosaurs had fairly small babies. Incredibly, some grown-up dinosaurs were 200 times bigger than their young. Experts aren't sure how fast the babies grew. Some may have taken as long as 20 years to grow to their full size.

On the right you can see a baby sauropod with its mother. Adults were absolutely huge, but babies were as small as cats. ★

Internet link

For a link to a website where you can see a video clip that shows how baby dinosaurs may have looked, go to **www.usborne-quicklinks.com**

Sea reptiles

While the dinosaurs lived on land, other prehistoric reptiles swam in the sea.

This sea reptile is called a plesiosaur.

Necks and flippers

Plesiosaurs were big sea reptiles with long necks and four paddle-shaped flippers. As they swam, they flapped their flippers slowly up and down like wings.

Liopleurodon was a gigantic pliosaur. It had the biggest jaws of any animal that ever lived.

Sea monsters

The biggest sea reptiles of all were the pliosaurs. These gigantic hunters had enormous jaws full of deadly teeth.

Breathing air

Most sea creatures can breathe underwater. But sea reptiles needed air to survive. They had to swim to the surface every now and then to take a gulp of air.

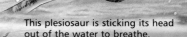

This plesiosaur is sticking its head out of the water to breathe.

Internet link

For a link to a website where you can see video clips of prehistoric sea reptiles, go to **www.usborne-quicklinks.com**

Expert swimmers

Ichthyosaurs were sea reptiles that looked like dolphins. They swam smoothly and quickly through the water. They moved around by swishing their tails from side to side.

Long, thin snout

Ichthyosaurs used their flippers to steer as they swam through the ocean.

As well as sea reptiles, there were lots of creatures with shells. This is an ammonite.

This is a pliosaur called Peloneustes. It could dive deep underwater.

Flying reptiles

Pterosaurs were reptiles with wings. They lived at the same time as the dinosaurs.

Different pterosaurs

Pterosaurs had wide, leathery wings and furry bodies. Some had long, bony tails and others had short tails. The smallest pterosaurs were the size of ducks, but the biggest ones were the size of a small plane.

Pterosaurs' wings were attached to their arms as well as to their bodies.

Pterodactylus had a short tail. This helped it to twist and turn in the air as it chased insects.

Pterodaustro had very fine teeth, like the bristles on a hairbrush. It scooped up water and trapped tiny sea creatures between its teeth.

Hollow bones

All pterosaurs had extremely light, hollow bones. This meant that even the biggest ones were light enough to get off the ground and stay in the air.

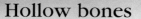

Quetzalcoatlus is the biggest pterosaur we know about.

Pterosaurs slept hanging upside down, like this.

Pteranodon had no teeth. It caught fish, then kept them in a pouch in its mouth. Later, it swallowed them whole.

Internet link

For a link to a website where you can find out more about Quetzalcoatlus, go to **www.usborne-quicklinks.com**

Fish eaters

Many pterosaurs ate insects, but some hunted fish and other sea creatures. They swooped down from the sky and snapped fish up from the water.

Rhamphorhynchus had a long tail. This helped to keep it steady in the air.

The death of the dinosaurs

About 65 million years ago, all the dinosaurs died out. Flying reptiles and most sea reptiles died out too. But how did this happen?

Deadly rock

65 million years ago, a giant rock, called a meteorite, came whizzing through space and smashed into the Earth. The meteorite was the size of a small town. Most experts think it was this meteorite that led to the dinosaurs dying out.

When the meteorite hit the Earth it made a huge explosion. This is how it may have looked.

Dust clouds

The meteorite broke into tiny pieces. For months, the world was surrounded by clouds of dust. Sunlight couldn't get through, so it was very cold and dark. This made it hard for animals to survive.

This shows what may have happened after the meteorite hit the Earth.

The air was full of dust. This made it hard to breathe.

Volcanoes

At the same time, lots of volcanoes in different parts of the world poured out red-hot lava (liquid rock) onto the Earth. The volcanoes also sent poisonous gases into the air. All of this made the world an even harder place to live in.

Here you can see lava pouring out of a volcano. Lava burns everything it touches.

Internet link

For a link to a website where you can see pictures of meteorites (or asteroids) and find out more, go to **www.usborne-quicklinks.com**

Strange survivors

Not all animals died out 65 million years ago. Lizards, snakes, birds and many other small creatures survived. Nobody knows why these animals didn't die out.

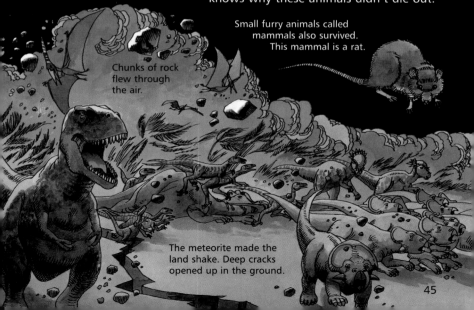

Small furry animals called mammals also survived. This mammal is a rat.

Chunks of rock flew through the air.

The meteorite made the land shake. Deep cracks opened up in the ground.

45

The first mammals

While the dinosaurs were alive, a group of animals called mammals also lived on the Earth. After the dinosaurs died out, new kinds of mammals began to appear. Slowly, they spread across the world.

This is a prehistoric mammal called Platybelodon.

★ This squirrel-like animal is called Ptilodus. It was one of the first mammals.

What is a mammal?

All mammals feed their babies with milk. They are also warm-blooded. This means they can make their own heat and stay warm even when it's cold. Most mammals are furry. Cats, horses and humans are mammals.

Below you can see some baby lions sucking milk from their mother.

★

Lots of mammals

There were many different kinds of prehistoric mammals. Some ate plants and others hunted animals. Most mammals lived on the ground, but some climbed trees, and some flew through the air. Others lived in the oceans.

Smilodectes was a small mammal that climbed trees.

★

Icaronycteris was one of the first bats.

Platybelodon was a kind of elephant. It had a wide, flat trunk.

Pointy tusk

Internet link

For a link to a website where you can see video clips of prehistoric mammals, go to **www.usborne-quicklinks.com**

Shovel-like teeth for scooping up food

More mammals

Some prehistoric mammals were meat-eaters that hunted other animals. Other early mammals only ate plants.

Hunters

Lots of the meat-eating mammals were a little like today's dogs, foxes and big cats. They were quick and cunning, and had excellent eyesight. They had long, pointy teeth and sharp claws for tearing up meat.

Smilodon was a tiger-like cat. It had two huge teeth.

Hunting in groups

Early dogs and wolves hunted in big groups, or packs. This meant they could kill animals much bigger than themselves.

These wolves are hunting an early camel called Titanotylopus.

The camel was bigger than camels are today.

The wolves surround the camel and close in on it slowly.

Staying safe

Plant-eating mammals had different ways of defending themselves against hunters.

Some plant-eaters had sharp horns on their heads. Some had long legs and could run fast, so they could escape from the meat-eaters. Many plant-eaters lived together in big herds to keep each other safe.

Brontotherium was a plant-eater with huge horns on its nose.

Antelopes were plant-eaters. This herd of antelopes is running away from a big cat.

Sharp horns for fighting off hunters

Internet link

For a link to a website where you can paint and print out a Smilodon, go to **www.usborne-quicklinks.com**

The antelopes had long legs, so they could run away from hunters.

49

South American mammals

Today, North and South America are joined together. But millions of years ago, South America was an island. Some of the mammals that lived there looked nothing like animals in other parts of the world.

Internet link

For a link to a website where you can find out more about Megatherium, go to **www.usborne-quicklinks.com**

Toxodon looked like a furry hippo.

Argyrolagus looked like a rat. It kept its babies in a pouch on its body, like a kangaroo.

Macrauchenia looked like a camel with a trunk.

Slow sloths

One group of strange South American mammals were the sloths. These plant-eaters had long, thick fur, and they moved very slowly. They couldn't run away from meat-eaters, but they had big, sharp claws to defend themselves.

On the left is a sloth called Megatherium. It was twice as big as a hippopotamus.

This is a modern-day sloth from South America. Today, sloths spend most of their time in the trees.

Bony domes

Glyptodonts were plant-eaters with thick, bony domes on top of their bodies. The domes protected them from meat-eaters.

Doedicurus was a glyptodont the size of a small car.

Doedicurus had a big spiky tail to defend itself against meat-eaters.

★

Ice age mammals

An ice age is a time when the weather gets colder all over the world. During an ice age, large parts of the Earth are covered in thick sheets of ice. This has happened several times since the Earth began.

Woolly rhinos like this one lived during the last ice age. They were covered in thick, shaggy hair.

Surviving the cold

The last ice age began 100,000 years ago. Many mammals left the icy places and went to live where it was warmer. All the mammals that stayed in the icy places grew very thick fur. This helped them to keep warm.

Here you can see some mammals that lived during the last ice age.

The arctic fox was a hunter. Its white fur helped it to hide in the snow.

★ Arctic hare

Reindeer lived in big herds. They had horns to defend themselves against meat-eating animals.

52

Woolly mammoths were elephants with thick hair all over their bodies.

Mammoths used their tusks to clear away snow and find plants to eat.

Internet link

For a link to a website where you can hear more about ice age mammals, go to **www.usborne-quicklinks.com**

Freezing wind blew snow across the icy plains.

After the ice age

The last ice age came to an end about 10,000 years ago. Many animals died out around this time. Experts think that the warmer weather made it hard for the ice age animals to survive. Lots of woolly mammoths and rhinos were killed by prehistoric people too.

53

The first people

For millions of years, there were no people on Earth. So where did people come from?

Just two legs

More than five million years ago, some apes in Africa started walking on two legs. Over a very long period of time, these apes turned into the first people on Earth.

This is Australopithecus, an ape that walked on two legs. It used its huge jaws for eating chewy grass and roots.

Changing people

The first people still looked a lot like apes. They had big jaws, and thick hair all over their bodies. Slowly, they became less hairy and their brains grew bigger. Over time, they learned how to make stone tools, light fires and talk to each other.

This scene shows how early people lived about two million years ago.

These men are bringing back animals they have killed.

These men are using wooden spears to catch fish.

People picked fruit and nuts to eat.

New people

People like us first lived on the Earth 150,000 years ago. They wandered from place to place, hunting animals and picking plants to eat.

People painted animals on cave walls. This painting of a horse is from a cave in France.

People used spears and stones to hunt deer and other animals for food.

Fire was useful for cooking meat and keeping warm.

Internet link

For a link to a website where you can play games, see video clips and find out more about the first people, go to **www.usborne-quicklinks.com**

People made simple knives by sharpening stones.

The first farmers

About 10,000 years ago, people started growing food and keeping animals. Instead of wandering around, they stayed on their farms. This was the beginning of village life.

How do we know?

Almost everything we know about prehistoric life comes from fossils. Fossils are parts of dead animals and plants that have been preserved under the ground.

★
A fossil of a sea creature called an ammonite

What are fossils?

When an animal dies, it usually rots away completely. But sometimes parts of a dead animal are hardened and become fossils. Here's how this happens.

An animal dies and its soft body rots away. Its skeleton is buried under layers of mud.

★

The mud slowly turns into stone. Chemicals from the stone drip down into tiny holes in the animal's bones.

★

The chemicals slowly harden inside the bones. Over a very long period of time, the skeleton turns into a fossil.

★

Here you can see a scientist chipping away rock to look at a fossil buried inside. Can you see the dinosaur's teeth?

Building an animal

When experts find fossils of a dead animal's bones, they can stick them back together to make a skeleton. This tells them how big the animal was and what shape its body was. Even if some bones are missing, they can still get a good idea of how the creature looked.

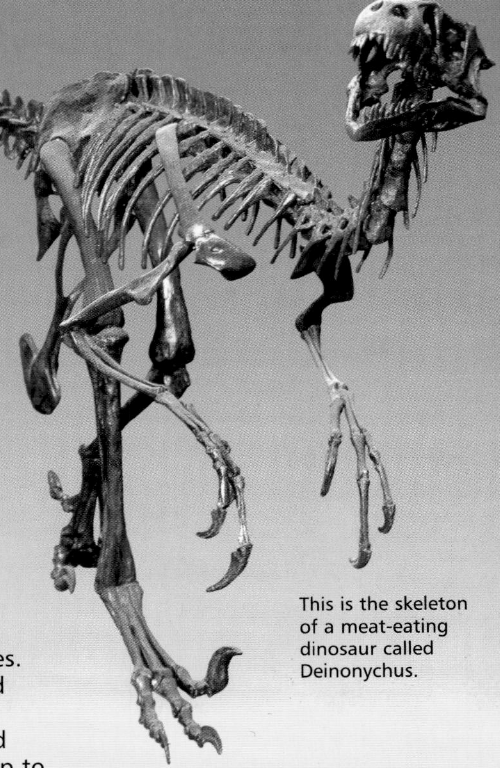

Internet link

For a link to a website where you can play a fossil matching game, go to **www.usborne-quicklinks.com**

Other fossils

Sometimes, the soft skin and muscles of a prehistoric animal were preserved as well as the bones. Footprints left by dinosaurs in mud were also preserved as the mud hardened. Experts have even found fossils of dinosaur dung. These help to show what the dinosaurs ate.

This is the skeleton of a meat-eating dinosaur called Deinonychus.

This picture shows a stegosaur and its baby walking through mud. The dinosaurs are leaving footprints behind them.

57

New discoveries

Even though dinosaurs died out millions of years ago, we are still finding out more about them. Experts all over the world discover new fossils all the time.

Four feathery wings

In 2002, experts in China found a fossil of a mysterious creature. It was a small, feathery dinosaur with four wings. This strange animal may have used its wings to glide between the branches of trees.

This dinosaur with four wings is called Microraptor.

Internet link

For a link to a website where you can see how people search for fossils, go to **www.usborne-quicklinks.com**

Rabbit teeth

Most dinosaurs that walked on two legs were fierce meat-eaters with teeth like knives. But a fossil found in 2002 shows a very different kind of two-legged dinosaur. It had big blunt teeth like a rabbit's, and it may have eaten plants instead of meat.

Incisivosaurus may have had feathers on its body and arms.

This is Incisivosaurus, a two-legged dinosaur which had rounded, rabbit-like teeth.

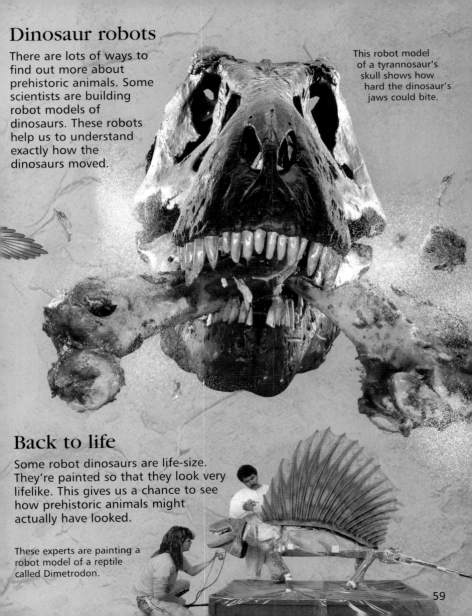

Dinosaur robots

There are lots of ways to find out more about prehistoric animals. Some scientists are building robot models of dinosaurs. These robots help us to understand exactly how the dinosaurs moved.

This robot model of a tyrannosaur's skull shows how hard the dinosaur's jaws could bite.

Back to life

Some robot dinosaurs are life-size. They're painted so that they look very lifelike. This gives us a chance to see how prehistoric animals might actually have looked.

These experts are painting a robot model of a reptile called Dimetrodon.

Prehistoric facts and figures

On this page are some facts and records about dinosaurs and other prehistoric animals.

First dinosaur: The first dinosaurs that we know about are Herrerasaurus and Eoraptor. These were fast-running meat-eaters that lived about 230 million years ago.

Smallest dinosaur: The smallest dinosaur we know about is Micropachycephalosaurus. It was 50cm (1½ft) long. This is only the size of a cat. Micropachycephalosaurus also holds another record. It's the dinosaur with the longest name – 23 letters long.

Shortest dinosaur name: A small plant-eating dinosaur with bony plates on its body has a name just five letters long – Minmi.

Biggest dinosaur: The biggest dinosaur we know about is called Argentinosaurus. This plant-eating giant may have been up to 50m (165ft) long. This is longer than two buses placed end to end.

Biggest meat-eating dinosaur: The biggest meat-eating dinosaur discovered so far is Giganotosaurus. This huge hunter was over 12m (40ft) long. This is even bigger than Tyrannosaurus rex.

Most intelligent dinosaur: The dinosaur with the biggest brain compared to the size of its body was Troodon. Troodon was a speedy meat-eater. Meat-eating dinosaurs were more intelligent than plant-eaters.

Least intelligent dinosaur: The dinosaur with the smallest brain compared to the size of its body was Apatosaurus, one of the huge plant-eating sauropods.

Oldest dinosaur: Enormous sauropods like Apatosaurus and Brachiosaurus probably lived to be 100 years old.

Fastest dinosaur: The fastest dinosaur was an ostrich dinosaur called Gallimimus. Experts think it could run as fast as a modern-day ostrich – about 56kph (35mph).

Longest tail: The dinosaur with the longest tail was a sauropod called Diplodocus. Its whip-like tail was 13m (43ft) long.

Longest neck: The dinosaur with the longest neck was Mamenchisaurus. Its neck was 15m (49ft) long.

Biggest head: A horned, plant-eating dinosaur called Torosaurus had the biggest skull of any land animal that has ever lived. Its head was almost 3m (10ft) long. If you turned it on its side and stood it on the ground, it would be taller than a person.

Longest claws: The dinosaur with the longest claws was Therizinosaurus. Its claws were 70cm (28in) long. Surprisingly, it was probably a plant-eater rather than a meat-eater. No one is sure why it had such big claws. It may have used them to defend itself against meat-eaters.

Biggest eggs: Sauropods laid the biggest eggs of any dinosaur. Their eggs were about 30cm (1ft) long. But this was still amazingly small compared to the gigantic size of the adult dinosaurs.

Biggest jaws: The creature with the biggest jaws ever was a sea reptile called Liopleurodon. Its jaws were 3m (10ft) long and its teeth were 30cm (1ft) long.

Biggest land mammal: The biggest mammal that ever lived on land was Indricotherium. This was a massive plant-eater that weighed as much as four elephants.

Prehistoric words

On this page, you can find out the meaning of some words used in this book and in other prehistoric books.

amphibian an animal that lives partly on land and partly in the water. Frogs and toads are amphibians.

carnivore an animal that only eats meat.

dinosaur a kind of prehistoric reptile. Dinosaurs died out 65 million years ago.

evolution the idea that living things slowly change over time.

extinct a word used to describe an animal or plant that has died out. Dinosaurs are extinct.

fossil the remains of a dead animal or plant preserved in rock.

fossilize turn into a fossil.

herbivore an animal that only eats plants.

herd a group of animals that live together.

ice age a period of time when it becomes very cold all over the world. The last ice age ended 10,000 years ago.

mammal an animal that feeds its babies with milk. Mammals are warm-blooded and most mammals have hair on their bodies. Dogs and humans are mammals.

omnivore an animal that eats both meat and plants.

palaeontologist a scientist who studies fossils to find out about prehistoric animals and plants.

raptor A meat-eating dinosaur that walked on two legs. Raptors had huge claws and were fierce hunters.

reptile an animal that has scaly skin, lays eggs and is cold-blooded. Lizards and snakes are reptiles.

scavenger an animal that eats meat from dead animals that it finds.

species a particular kind of plant or animal. Lions are one species and tigers are another.

This is a pliosaur, a sea reptile that lived at the same time as the dinosaurs.

Index

Acknowledgements

The publishers are grateful to the following for permission to reproduce material:

Key
t = top, m = middle, b = bottom, l = left, r = right

Cover (main image) ©Kokoro Company Ltd.; (background) ©Digital Vision; (dragonfly) ©Peter Johnson/CORBIS; p5 ©Joe McDonald/CORBIS; pp6-7 ©Mark Garlick/Science Photo Library; p7tr ©Sinclair Stammers/Science Photo Library; p9 (coral) ©Digital Vision; p12 ©Ron Holthuysen Scientific Art Studio; p13 ©Dr George C. McGavin/Oxford University Museum of Natural History; p14l ©David A. Northcott/CORBIS; p14br ©NHPA/Daniel Heuclin; p16 ©1997, Carlos Papolio; p18tl ©2003, Griffon Enterprises; p18b ©Gary Staab; p18 (background) ©Digital Vision; p19 ©Kokoro Company Ltd.; pp20-21 ©Alan Groves; p22bl ©Alan Groves; pp22-23 ©Oxford University Museum of Natural History; p23 ©James L. Amos/CORBIS; p24 ©Kokoro Company Ltd.; p25 ©Kokoro Company Ltd.; pp24-25 (background) ©Digital Vision; p28 ©Kokoro Company Ltd.; p29 ©Kokoro Company Ltd.; pp28-29 (ferns) ©Digital Vision; pp30-31 ©Kokoro Company Ltd.; pp32-33 (stegosaurs) ©Kokoro Company Ltd.; pp32-33 (background) ©Digital Vision; p35 ©All rights reserved, Image Archives, Denver Museum of Nature and Science; pp36-37 (all dinosaurs) ©Kokoro Company Ltd.; pp36-37 (background) ©Digital Vision; p38tl ©The Natural History Museum, London; pp38-39 ©The Natural History Museum, London; p40 (Liopleurodon) ©Oxford University Museum of Natural History; p41 (ichthyosaur) ©Ron Holthuysen Scientific Art Studio; pp40-41 (background) ©Digital Vision; pp42-43 (background) ©Digital Vision; p44 ©Digital Vision (digital manipulation by Wychnet ICT Solutions); p45 ©Kevin Schafer/CORBIS; pp46-47 (elephant) ©Kokoro Company Ltd.; p46-47 (background) ©Digital Vision; p49 ©Ron Holthuysen Scientific Art Studio; p51 ©Michael and Patricia Fogden/CORBIS; p52 (rhino) ©Kokoro Company Ltd.; p53 (mammoth) ©Kokoro Company Ltd.; pp52-53 (background) ©Digital Vision; p54 ©BOSSU REGIS/CORBIS SYGMA; p55 ©Bettmann/CORBIS; p56 ©Jonathan Blair/CORBIS; p57 ©The Natural History Museum, London; pp58-59 (background) ©Digital Vision; p59t ©Robert Caputo/AURORA; p59b ©Peter Menzel, Dinamation/Science Photo Library.

Additional design: Stephanie Jones
Digital image manipulation: Keith Newell, Mark Franklin, John Russell and Wychnet ICT Solutions
Additional artwork: Ian Jackson, John Hughes and Inklink Firenze
Additional photography: MMStudios
Editor: Fiona Chandler
Additional research: Ruth King and Claire Masset
Editorial director: Felicity Brooks
Art director: Mary Cartwright

Every effort has been made to trace and acknowledge ownership of copyright. If any rights have been omitted, the publishers offer to rectify this in any subsequent editions following notification.